Chhath Puja: Bihar's Sacred Ritual of Sun Worship

"As the first rays of dawn break over the riverbanks of Bihar, thousands of devotees stand knee-deep in water, hands folded in reverence to the Sun God, Surya. The air is thick with devotion, echoing with ancient hymns and the soft sound of lapping water—a tribute to the celestial energy that sustains all life."

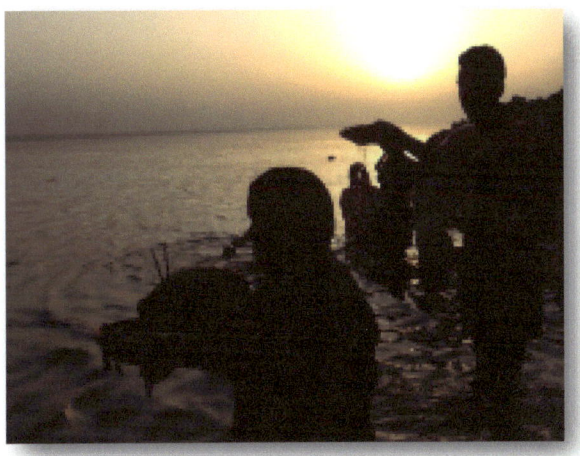

Chhath Puja is much more than a festival; it is a living tradition that binds people across generations and distances in an intense expression of faith and gratitude.

Celebrated with unparalleled devotion, Chhath Puja is a four-day journey of worship, purification, and self-discipline that pays homage to Surya, the giver of light, and Chhathi Maiya, the divine mother.

Rooted in Bihar's cultural heart, this sacred ritual invites devotees to connect deeply with nature, offering prayers at the water's edge at sunrise and sunset.

Each moment of Chhath is filled with reverence, as families gather to honor the cycle of life and renew their bonds to the earth and sky.

This is the spirit of Chhath Puja—a celebration of life, legacy, and light.

Chapter 1: Origins and Significance of Chhath Puja

> "Om Hrim Hrim Suryaya Namah"
>
> — A Vedic Chant to Surya, the Sun God

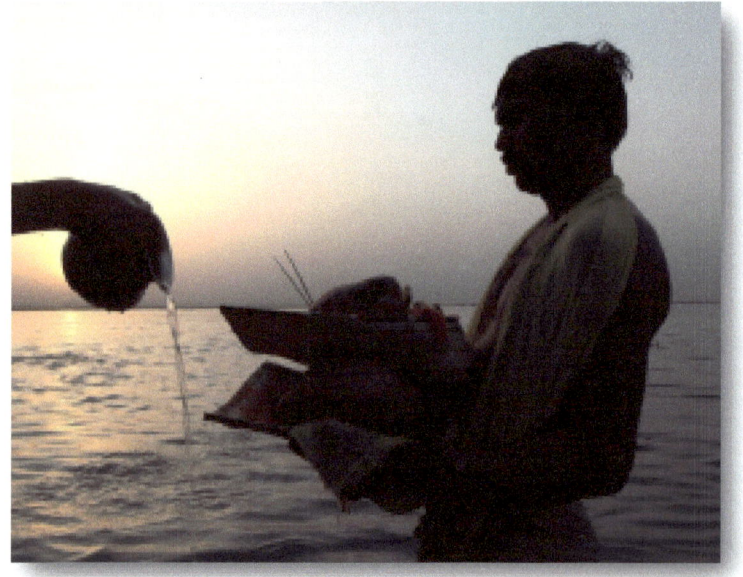

The ancient chant resounds with reverence, paying homage to Surya, the divine force that lights the world and nourishes life.

Surya is more than a celestial body; in Vedic tradition, he embodies the life-giving energy that sustains nature, humans, and all creatures.

To honor Surya is to acknowledge our interconnectedness with the cosmos, to give thanks for the warmth, vitality, and abundance that flow from the Sun.

History and Origins of Chhath Puja

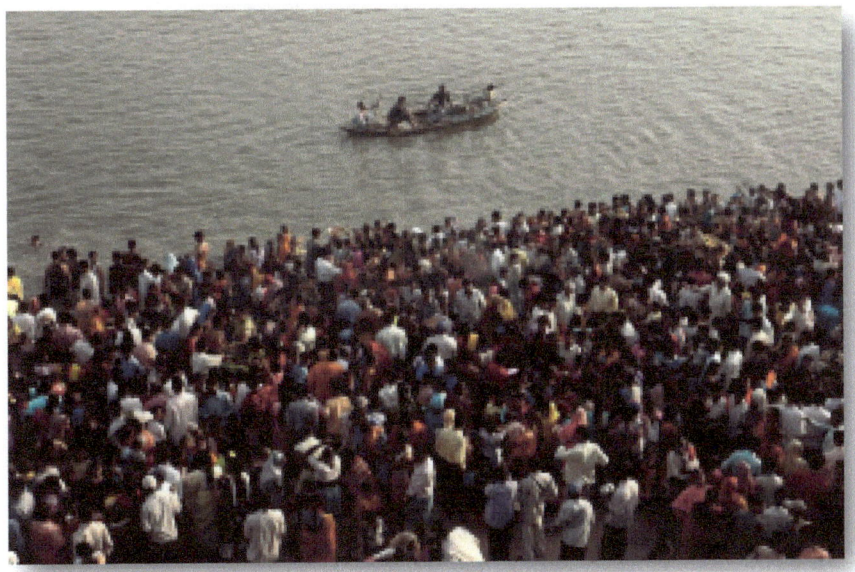

The origins of Chhath Puja can be traced back to the Vedic period, when sun worship held profound significance in early Hindu scriptures.

This ancient festival is mentioned in the *Rigveda*, where hymns dedicated to Surya illuminate his divine status as a source of light, life, and spiritual power.

Historical records reveal that Chhath Puja is possibly one of the oldest forms of sun worship, with roots that reach into the heart of Bihar's rich spiritual traditions.

Manish Sinha

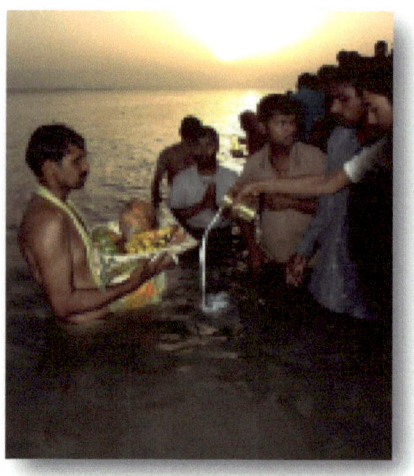

In ancient times, sun worship was not only an act of faith but also a means of connecting with the rhythm of nature.

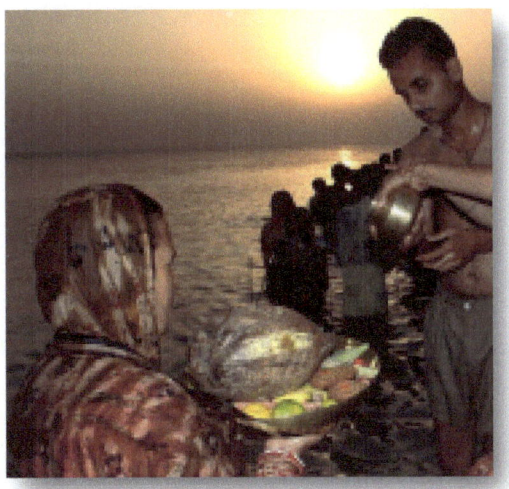

The festival of Chhath Puja evolved as a community observance, where families would come together by riverbanks to offer gratitude to Surya and seek his blessings for health, prosperity, and well-being.

This ancient practice, preserved for generations, is evident in Bihar's enduring reverence for water bodies, especially rivers, as sacred sites of devotion.

Close to Bihar's cultural roots, the festival has grown through time to embody values of purity, discipline, and unity, uniting families, villages, and entire communities.

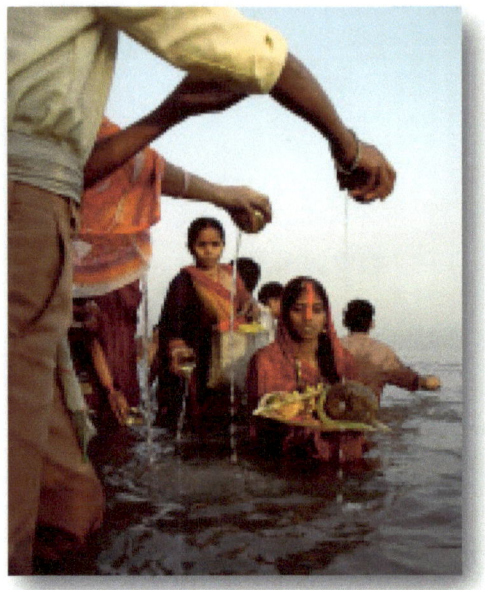

Visual representations of Surya—depicted riding a chariot drawn by seven horses—adorn temples across Bihar, reminding people of the timeless importance of Chhath Puja.

These symbols, etched in stone and revered in hearts, reflect an eternal bond between the Sun and his devotees.

Significance of Sun Worship and Connection to Chhathi Maiya

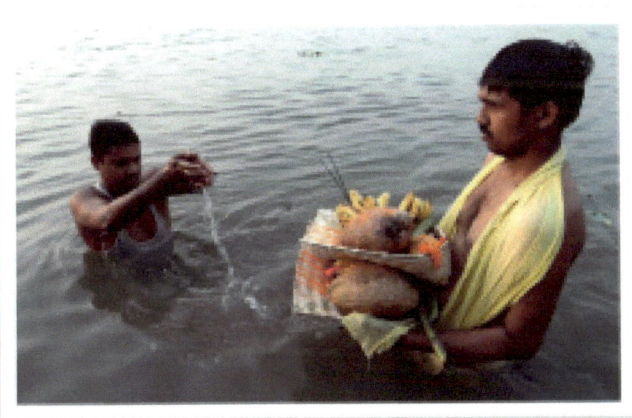

In Chhath Puja, Surya is worshipped not merely as a physical entity but as a divine energy, a source of healing and spiritual enlightenment.

The practice of sun worship holds both religious and ecological significance, emphasizing respect for natural elements.

Devotees believe that worshipping Surya directly benefits mental and physical health, a notion supported by modern science, which recognizes the Sun's crucial role in vitality and well-being.

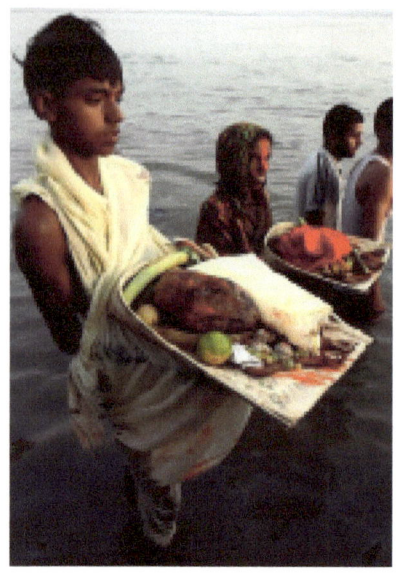 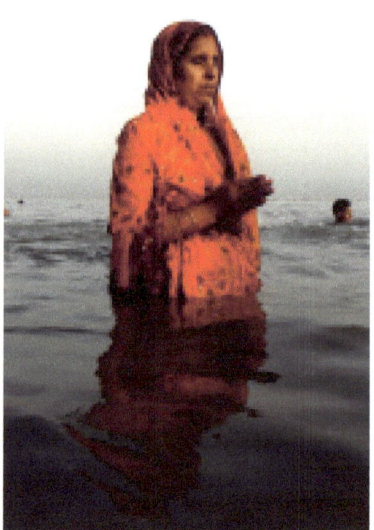

Central to Chhath Puja is the worship of Chhathi Maiya, the goddess who is believed to bestow blessings of fertility, prosperity, and protection.

Known as a benevolent maternal figure, Chhathi Maiya embodies the nurturing aspects of life, caring for families and ensuring harmony in the home.

The synergy of honoring both Surya and Chhathi Maiya symbolizes the balance between masculine and feminine energies, sun and earth, strength and compassion.

For the people of Bihar, Chhath Puja is an occasion to connect with these divine forces at a deeply personal level.

As they stand in the river, offering *arghya* (offerings of water and prayers) to the rising and setting sun, worshippers experience a moment of transcendence, a silent communion with the natural world.

This ritual, guided by ancient chants and personal devotion, reaffirms humanity's humble place within the cosmos and highlights a tradition that has endured and evolved but never wavered in its reverence for life and light.

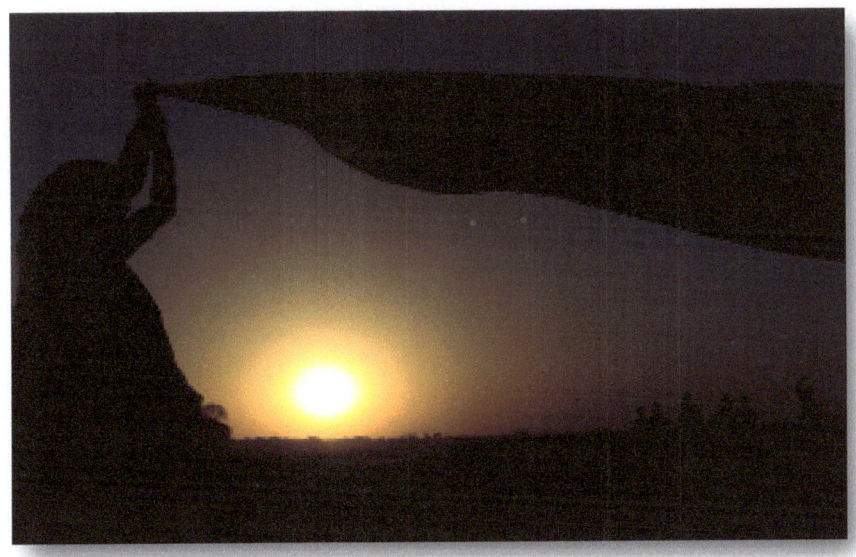

Chapter 2: The Four-Day Rituals

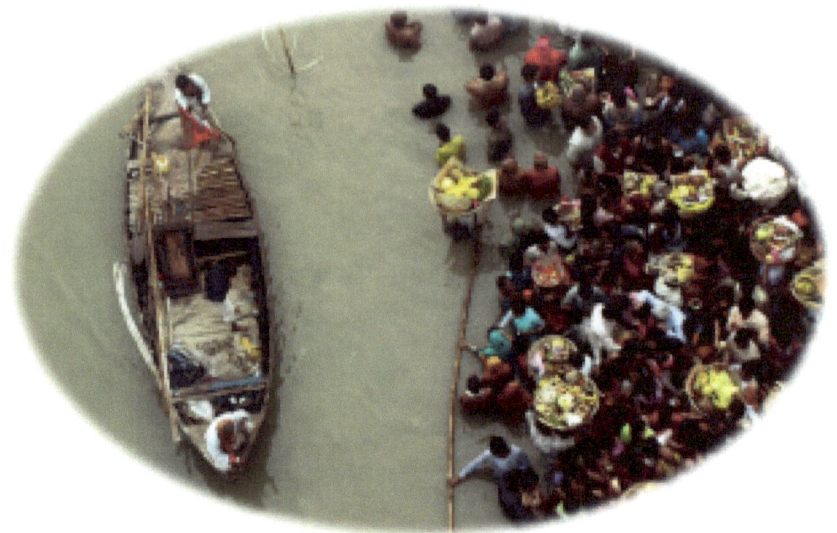

Nahay Khay – The First Day of Purification

"Nahay Khay – The Cleansing of the Body and Spirit"

Nahay Khay, the first day of Chhath Puja, marks the beginning of the devotee's journey of purification and devotion.

"Nahay" means to bathe, and "Khay" means to eat.

Chhath Puja: Bihar's Sacred Ritual of Sun Worship

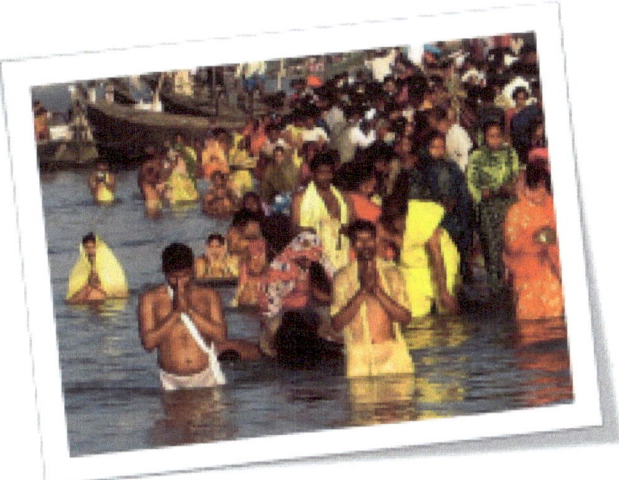

This day is dedicated to **physical and spiritual cleansing**, setting the tone for the days to come.

The devotees immerse themselves in this ritual with humility and reverence, believing that purity of body and mind will prepare them to connect more deeply with Surya and Chhathi Maiya.

Families gather to wash away impurities, both internal and external, in preparation for the sacred days ahead.

The ritual begins with a sacred bath, usually in a river, pond, or nearby water body, symbolizing a return to nature and an act of cleansing.

After bathing, devotees return home to prepare a simple, satvik meal, made with great care and purity.

Traditionally, this meal excludes any ingredients that are considered impure or heavy, focusing on foods like rice, pumpkin, and dal cooked in earthen pots.

The entire family joins in the preparation and consumption of this meal, symbolizing unity, simplicity, and devotion.

The Sacred Bath – Embracing Nature's Purity

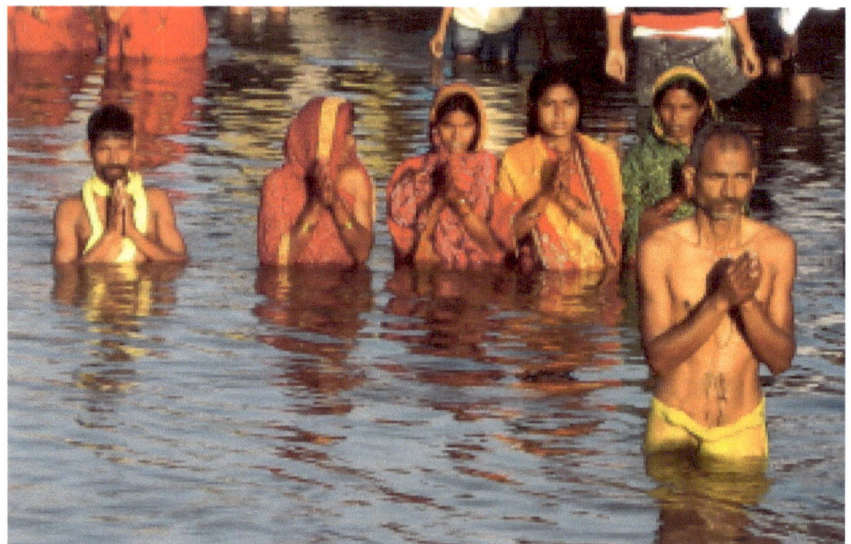

> "Devotees stand in reverence, immersed in the holy waters during the sacred bath of Chhath Puja, as they embrace nature's purity and offer prayers to the Sun God at dawn."

For many, this is more than a physical cleansing;

it is a spiritual connection to the natural world.

This sacred bath symbolizes the washing away of impurities, a moment of surrender to nature's purifying essence.

The scene reflects harmony between the people and their environment, reminding us of our shared bond with the water and earth.

Family Gatherings – A Ritual of Unity

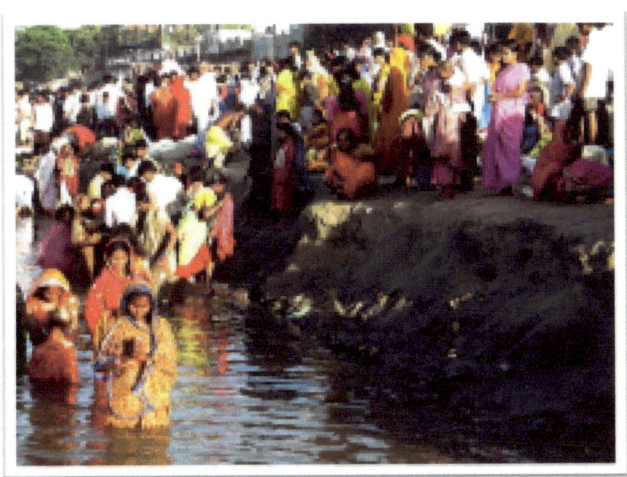

> "Nahay Khay is not only an individual's journey of purification but a family's collective ritual, bringing everyone together in devotion. It is a reminder that Chhath Puja is a festival of unity, where each family member plays a part in preparing for the sacred days ahead."

Women clean and prepare rice, dal, and vegetables with great attention, while children watch, eager to participate in this sacred tradition.

The atmosphere is one of warmth, devotion, and anticipation, where family bonds are strengthened as they come together in shared purpose.

Cooking in Earthen Pots – A Return to Simplicity

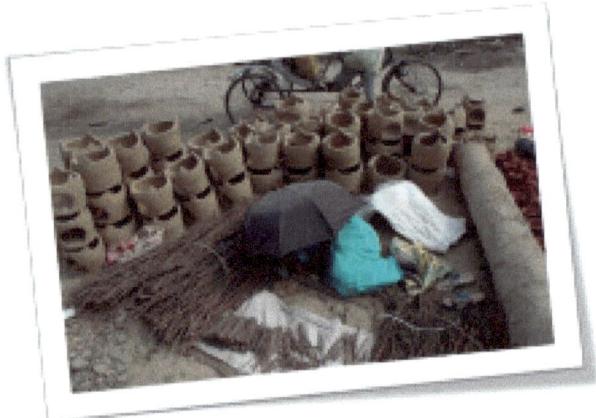

"Cooking in earthen pots is a tribute to tradition, purity, and simplicity. These pots are believed to carry the essence of the earth, infusing the meal with a deeper sense of connection to the divine."

The use of earthenware connects devotees to their roots and serves as an offering of humility to the divine.

Cooking in these vessels is symbolic of going back to nature, as the clay from the earth is believed to add purity to the meal.

The simplicity of the meal reflects the festival's focus on purity, abstaining from lavish ingredients to honor Chhath's values of humility and restraint.

The Satvik Meal – A Taste of Devotion

Chhath Puja: Bihar's Sacred Ritual of Sun Worship

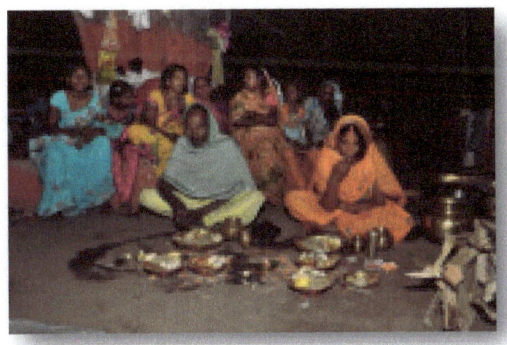

"The satvik meal on Nahay Khay is more than sustenance; it is a humble offering to one's body and spirit. Devotees partake in this meal to cleanse from within, preparing themselves for the days of fasting and devotion."

The food, served with reverence, symbolizes the purity and minimalism that guide every aspect of Chhath Puja.

Each bite is an offering to the self, a quiet act of gratitude, and a step toward physical and mental discipline.

The simplicity of the meal—void of spices and extravagance—reflects the spirit of humility and gratitude that Chhath Puja cultivates.

Kharna – The Day of Fasting and Devotion

"Kharna – A Day of Fasting, Faith, and Offering"

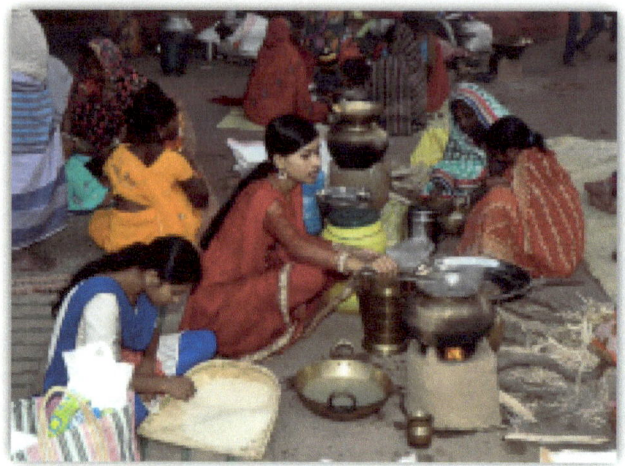

Kharna, the second day of Chhath Puja, is a day of intense devotion and gratitude, marked by a ritual fast and the preparation of a special offering.

On this day, devotees observe a strict fast from sunrise until they make offerings to Chhathi Maiya in the evening.

It is a practice of discipline, purity, and devotion, where even a sip of water is avoided until the evening prayer.

As night falls, devotees prepare a simple, sacred meal as an offering, which is later shared among family and community members.

This ritual not only signifies spiritual cleansing but also strengthens communal bonds, as the family gathers to prepare and partake in the prasad.

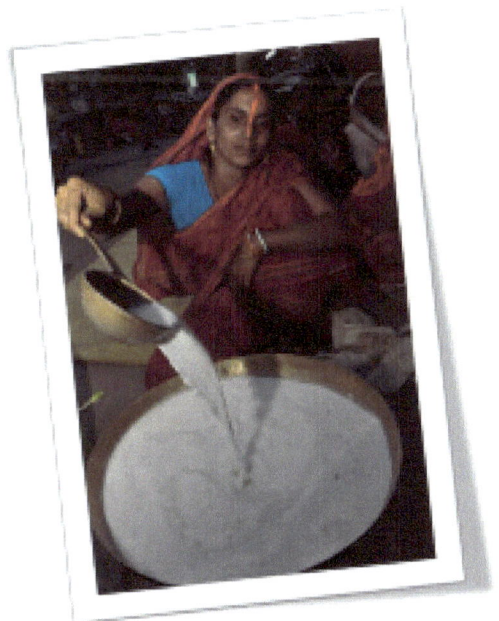

Preparing Prasad – A Ritual of Devotion

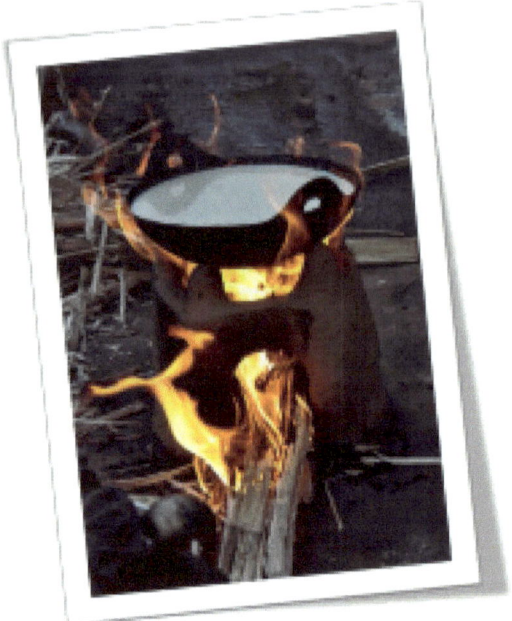

"Kharna prasad is prepared with deep reverence, as each step in the process is seen as an offering to the divine. The sweetness of the kheer and the earthiness of the thekua symbolize the joy and purity devotees bring to Chhath Puja."

The main items for the prasad are rice kheer (a sweet rice pudding) made with jaggery, milk, and ghee, along with thekua, a traditional wheat flour and jaggery biscuit.

Each ingredient is chosen for its simplicity and purity, representing the values of humility and devotion that Kharna embodies.

Offering the Prasad – A Sacred Act of Gratitude

Chhath Puja: Bihar's Sacred Ritual of Sun Worship

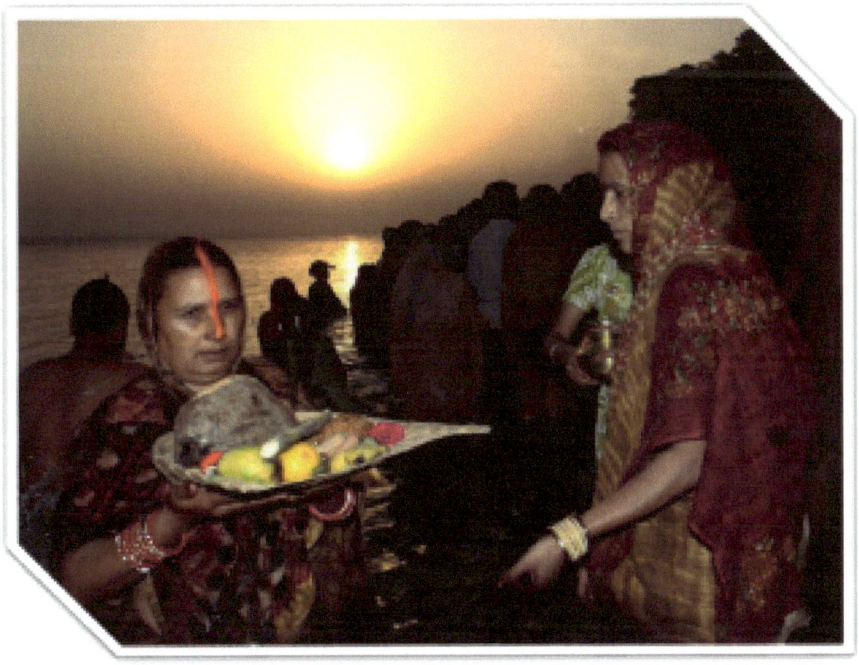

"With folded hands and a bowed head, the devotee offers the prasad to Chhathi Maiya, expressing gratitude for the goddess's blessings. It is a quiet, sacred moment, where worldly concerns are set aside in favor of faith and devotion."

This act of offering is the highlight of Kharna, a moment of silent prayer and gratitude.

Devotees express their thanks to the goddess for her blessings, asking for continued prosperity, health, and happiness for their family and community.

Breaking the Fast – A Moment of Communion

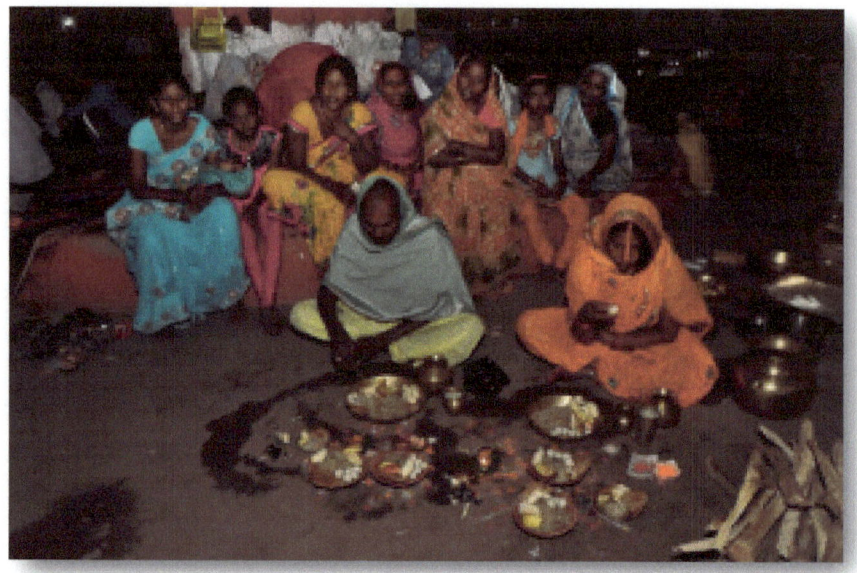

"After offering the prasad, the fast is broken with a shared meal, as family and friends gather to partake in the blessed food. This simple act of eating together strengthens communal bonds and reflects the values of harmony and gratitude at the heart of Chhath Puja."

After the offering is made, devotees break their fast by consuming the prasad, which is seen as blessed food.

The entire family partakes in the meal together, reinforcing bonds and creating a shared sense of purpose and devotion.

Children, elders, and family members all join in this meal, emphasizing the importance of unity in Chhath Puja.

The Spiritual Significance of Kharna

Chhath Puja: Bihar's Sacred Ritual of Sun Worship

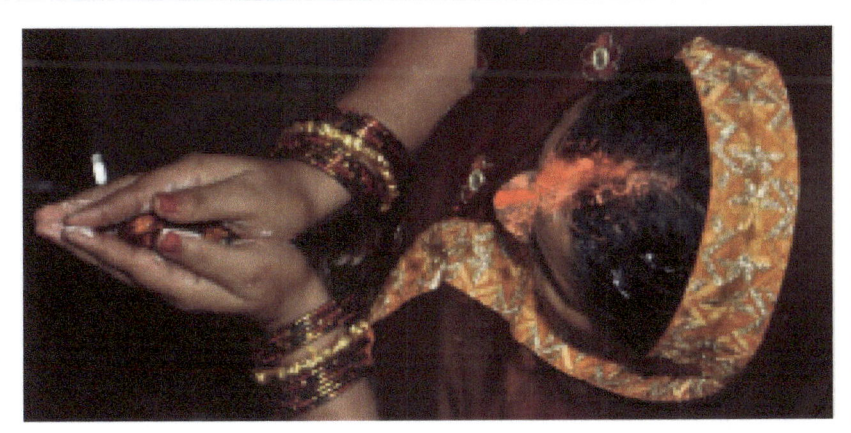

"Kharna represents the heart of Chhath Puja's spiritual journey—a day of purification, humility, and devotion that renews the mind and spirit. Through fasting and prayer, devotees strengthen their resolve and deepen their connection to the divine, paving the way for the days of devotion yet to come."

The day's fasting and preparation, culminating in the evening offering, is more than a ritual—it is a journey of self-discipline and faith.

Kharna embodies the spirit of simplicity, humility, and unwavering devotion to Chhathi Maiya and Surya, serving as a preparation for the grand offerings of the following days.

Sandhya Arghya – Evening Worship to the Setting Sun

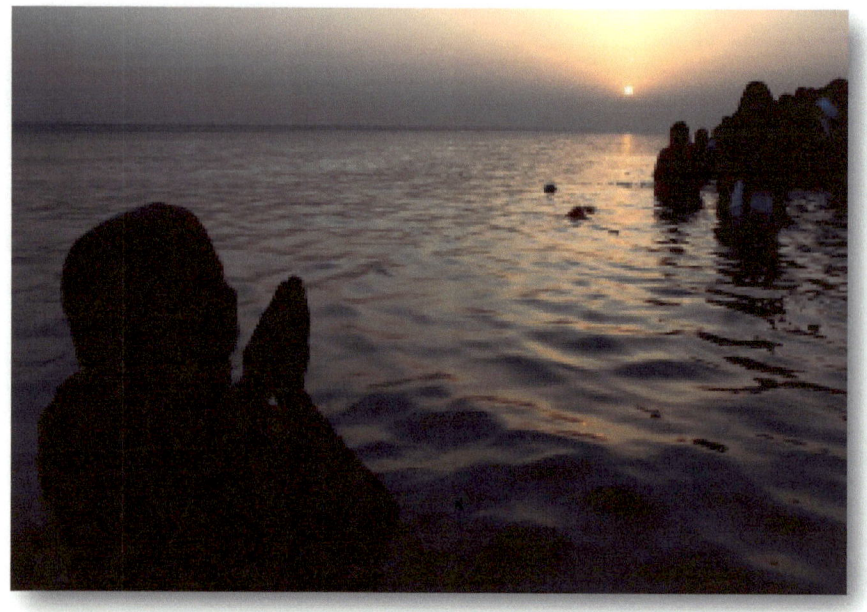

"Sandhya Arghya – Honoring the Sun's Journey into the Night"

Sandhya Arghya, or the Evening Offering, is one of the most powerful moments in the Chhath Puja festival.

On this third day, devotees gather by rivers, ponds, and other water bodies at dusk to offer their prayers to the setting sun.

This ritual is a profound act of gratitude, where worshippers thank Surya, the Sun God, for blessing them with life, warmth, and sustenance.

With folded hands, offerings in hand, and hearts full of devotion, they stand knee-deep in water, facing the sun as it dips below the horizon.

Sunset Over the Water – A Golden Embrace

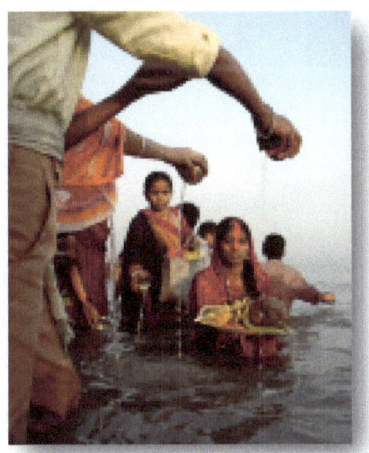

"As the sun begins its descent, a tranquil silence fills the air, and devotees gather to give thanks. The sunset reflects the beauty and balance of nature, reminding us of the Sun God's life-giving light and our own journey of devotion."

The soft hues of orange, pink, and purple create a serene and sacred atmosphere, enhancing the feeling of unity between humans and the natural world.

The sun, gradually descending toward the horizon, mirrors the devotees' humility as they honor its journey into the night.

Devotees in Prayer – An Act of Deep Reverence

Manish Sinha

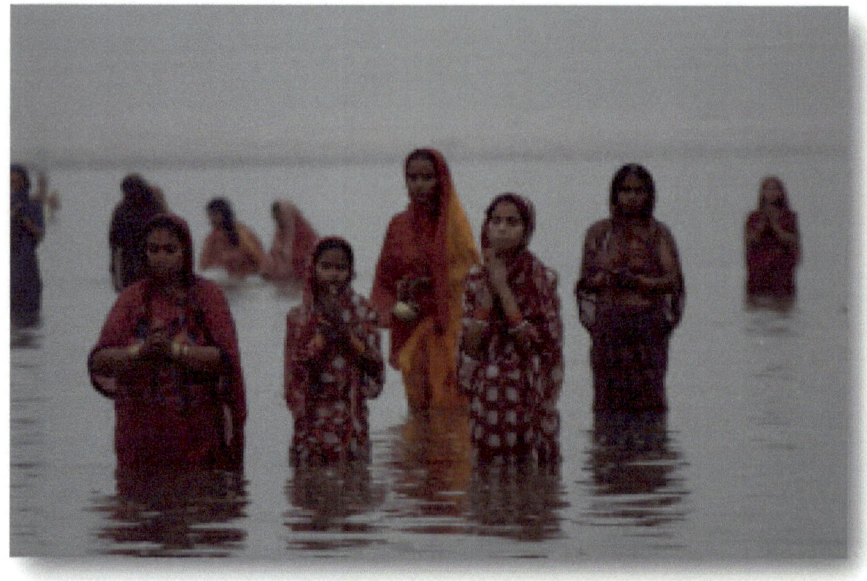

"With hands folded and eyes closed, devotees make their offering to Surya, seeking blessings for health, prosperity, and peace. In these moments of silent prayer, they find solace and strength, united by a shared faith."

The intense concentration on their faces reveals the depth of their faith and connection to the divine.

Each gesture, from the folding of hands to the holding of the diya, embodies the humility and gratitude with which they approach this sacred moment.

Families United in Devotion – Generations at Worship

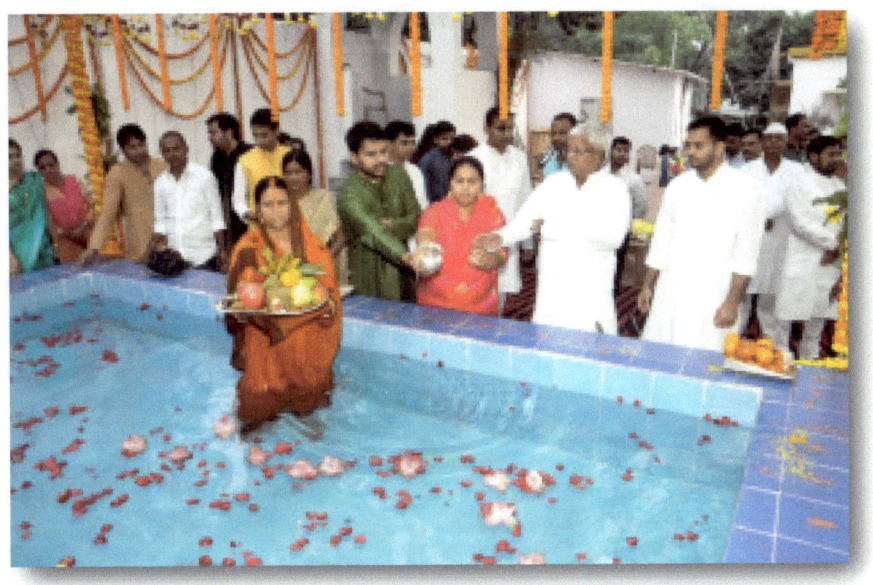

"In the soft glow of sunset, families come together to worship, sharing in the sacredness of the moment. The unity of generations paying homage to Surya speaks to the timeless importance of Chhath Puja and the strength of familial bonds."

Parents, children, and grandparents all stand side by side, offering their prayers together as the sun sets.

The presence of different generations reflects how the values and traditions of Chhath Puja are passed down, year after year, creating a legacy of faith and devotion that spans lifetimes.

The Spiritual Connection – A Moment of Transcendence

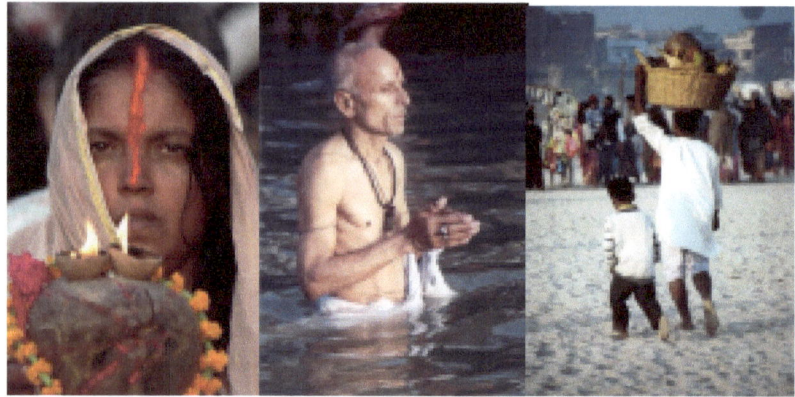

"As the sun dips below the horizon, devotees are enveloped in a sense of peace and fulfillment. In this moment of transcendence, they find a connection to something greater than themselves—a connection that renews their faith, strengthens their spirit, and prepares them for the dawn of a new day."

This scene encapsulates the spirituality of Sandhya Arghya, where worshippers feel a profound connection with the universe.

As the sun sets, they are left in quiet contemplation, holding on to the blessings of the day and preparing for the morning offering that awaits.

Usha Arghya – Morning Worship to the Rising Sun

Chhath Puja: Bihar's Sacred Ritual of Sun Worship

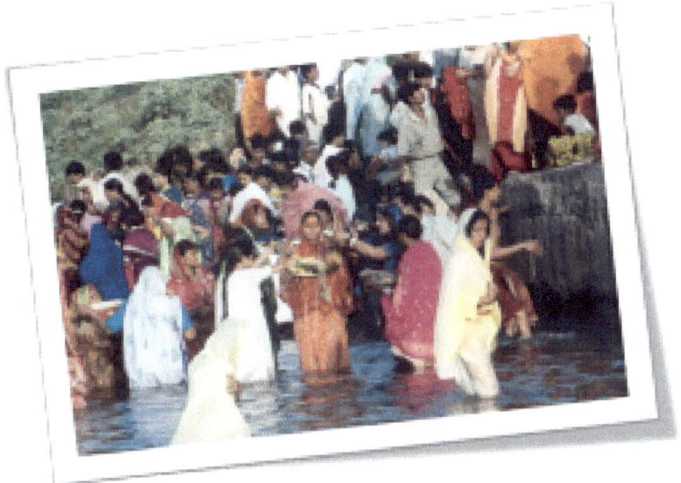

"Usha Arghya – Welcoming the Sun's First Rays with Devotion"

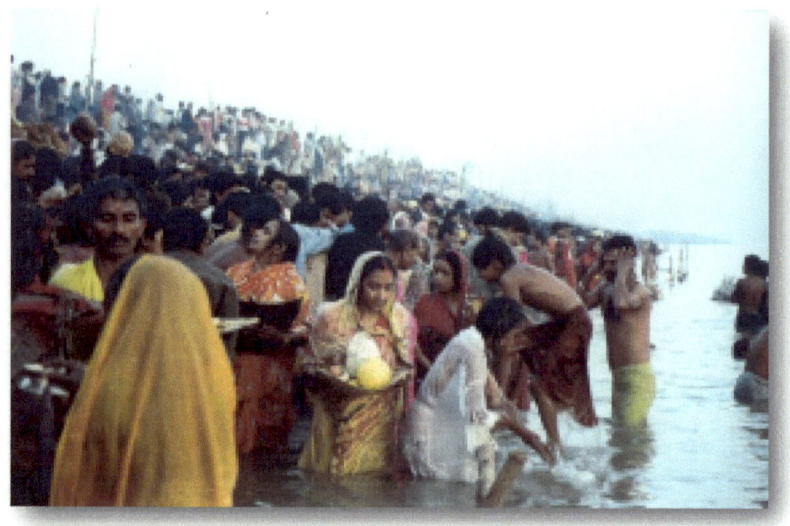

Usha Arghya, or the Morning Offering, is the culminating ritual of Chhath Puja.

On this final day, devotees gather at the break of dawn to offer prayers to the rising sun, symbolizing hope, renewal, and the promise of a new beginning.

The morning worship is a moment of immense joy and reverence as worshippers stand in the water, holding their offerings aloft, their faces illuminated by the first light of day.

The rising sun represents Surya's power to dispel darkness and bestow blessings, embodying both the literal and symbolic renewal of life.

This morning arghya signifies the end of the devotees' journey of devotion, fasting, and prayer, as they seek blessings for health, happiness, and prosperity.

Usha Arghya captures the spirit of resilience and optimism, as each person finds strength and peace in the radiant glow of dawn.

Chhath Puja: Bihar's Sacred Ritual of Sun Worship

This ritual reminds devotees of the cyclical nature of existence, and that every end is but a new beginning blessed by the grace of Surya.

The First Light – A Sacred Dawn

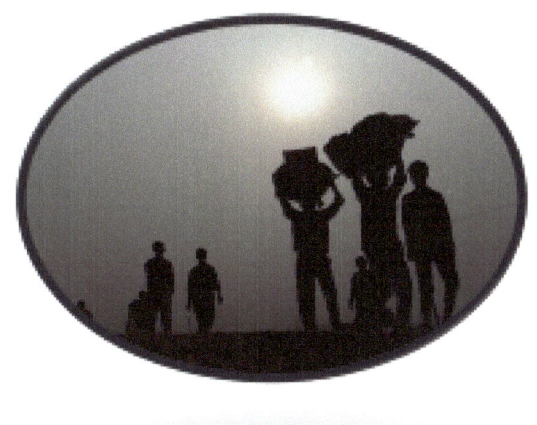

"As the sun rises, the world is bathed in a soft, sacred light, and devotees stand in reverence. This first light symbolizes new beginnings, filling the worshippers with hope and gratitude for the journey they've completed."

The soft pinks and oranges of the early morning sky create a serene, ethereal atmosphere, amplifying the feeling of renewal.

Devotees stand quietly in the water, eyes closed or fixed on the horizon, welcoming the first light of day with hearts full of gratitude.

Hands Raised in Offering – An Expression of Faith

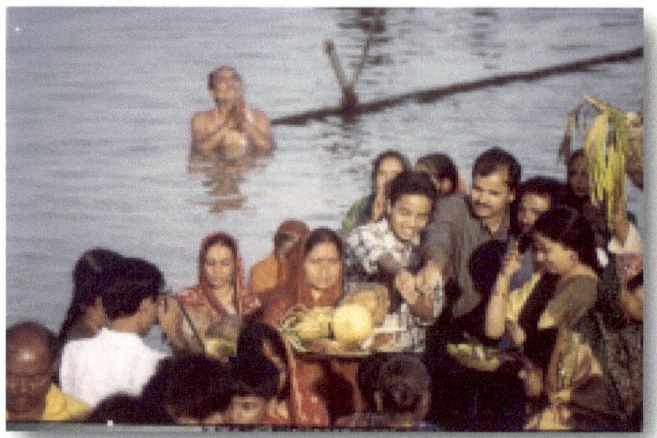

"With offerings held high, worshippers offer their heartfelt prayers to Surya. This humble act of devotion is a reminder of their gratitude for life's blessings and their hope for the Sun God's guidance and protection."

The diya, glowing faintly against the backdrop of the rising sun, represents the worshipper's inner light and their faith in Surya's blessings.

The simple yet profound act of offering symbolizes humility, devotion, and a heart that seeks the divine.

Families Gathered in Unity – The Bonds of Devotion

Chhath Puja: Bihar's Sacred Ritual of Sun Worship

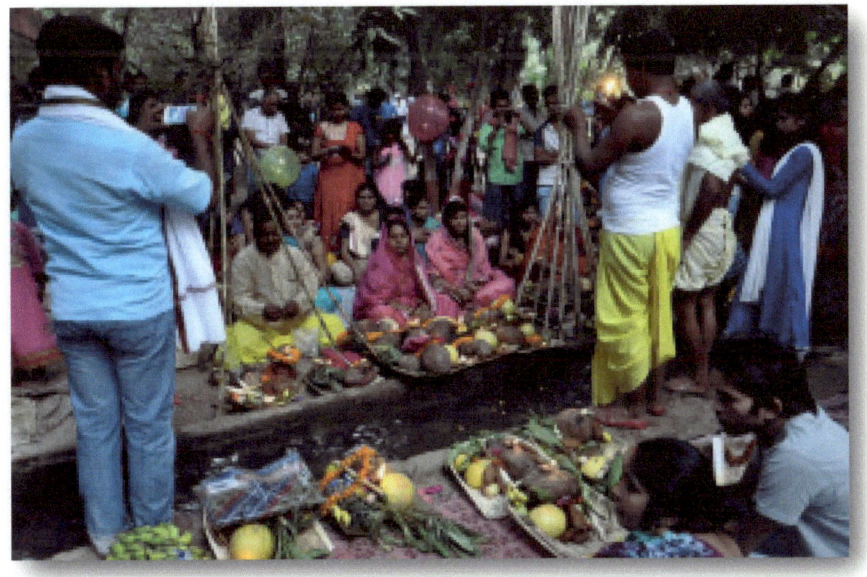

"In the early morning light, families gather in reverence, passing down the rituals of Chhath Puja from generation to generation. The rising sun brings with it a sense of unity, grounding each family in faith and tradition."

The family members wear traditional attire, and their faces reflect the peace and joy that comes with fulfilling the rituals of Chhath Puja.

This scene reflects the continuity of culture and faith, as each generation participates in the act of honoring Surya.

The Rising Sun – A Symbol of Hope and Renewal

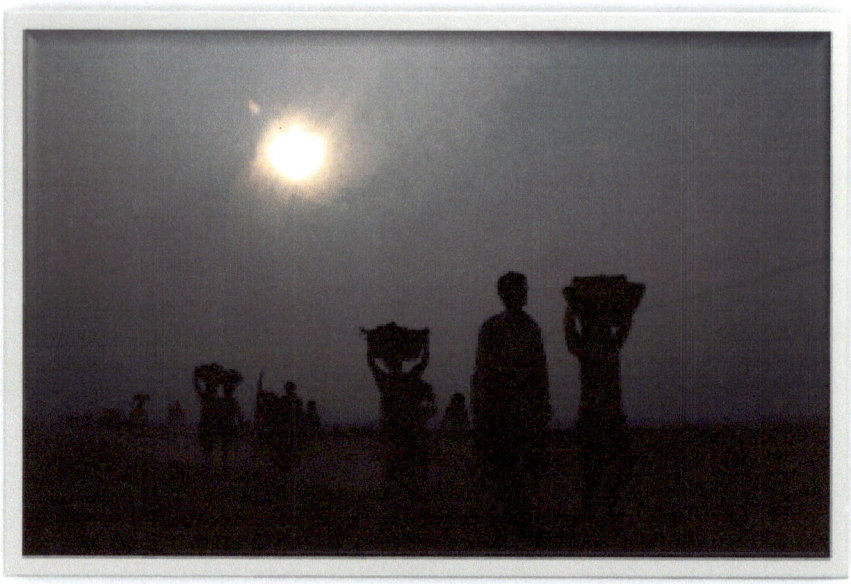

"Devotees carry offerings at dawn, silhouetted against the rising sun—a powerful emblem of hope, renewal, and devotion in the sacred ritual of Chhath Puja."

This image captures the essence of Usha Arghya, as the warmth of the sun symbolizes new hope and endless possibilities.

Devotees stand with serene expressions, feeling a profound connection to the divine and a sense of peace as they conclude their prayerful journey.

Chapter 3: Offerings and Prasad – Symbols of Devotion and Community

Chhath Puja: Bihar's Sacred Ritual of Sun Worship

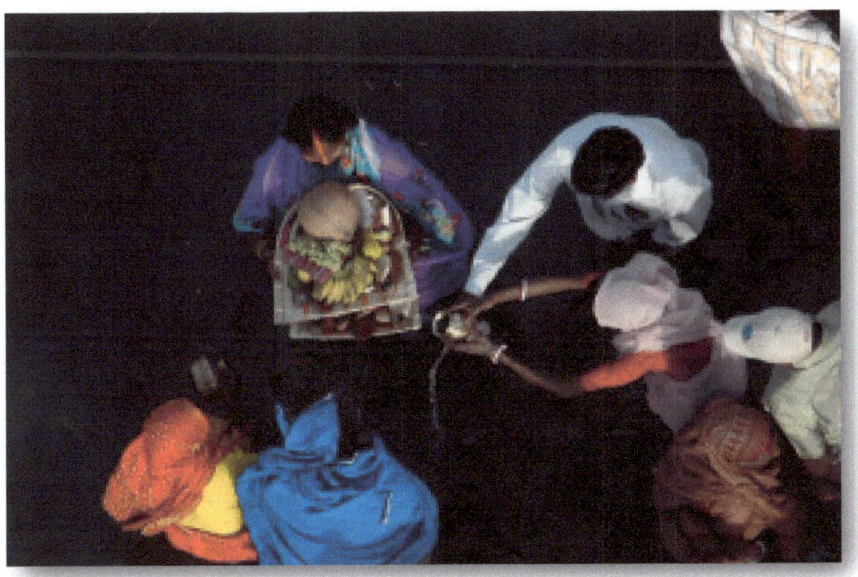

The offerings in Chhath Puja are more than mere items;

they are symbols of gratitude, purity, and devotion presented to the Sun God, Surya, and Chhathi Maiya.

Each offering, or prasad, holds a unique meaning and embodies the simplicity and sanctity of the ritual.

Hand-prepared with dedication and care, the prasad items are crafted using traditional methods, reflecting the deep-rooted connection between devotees and nature.

These sacred offerings are not only an expression of worship but also serve as a medium of unity, bringing together families and communities in a collective act of devotion.

Sacred Offerings of Devotion: Symbols of Faith and Gratitude

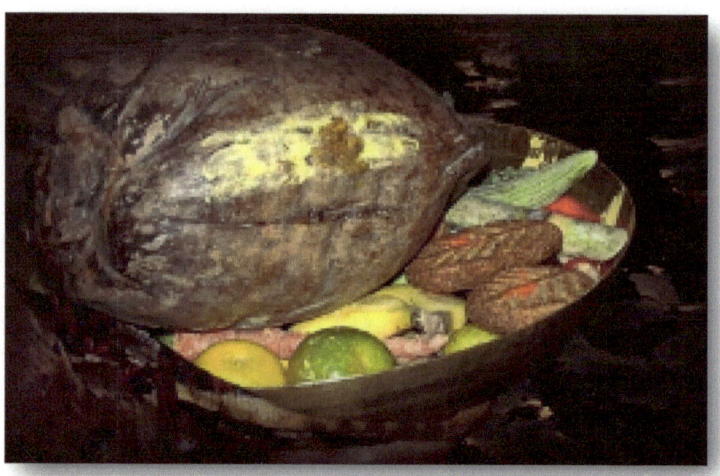

> "Thekua, a humble yet deeply symbolic sweet, captures the true spirit of Chhath Puja. It is a humble tribute to nature's bounty, crafted with ingredients that are both nourishing and symbolic of the devotees' connection to their roots."

Chhath Puja's offerings hold profound symbolism, each item a tribute to the Earth's bounty and the faith of the devotees.

The *thekua*, with its golden-brown color and intricate patterns, is the signature offering of this festival.

Made from simple ingredients like wheat flour, jaggery, and ghee, it embodies the richness of nature and the humility of those who prepare it.

Lovingly crafted by hand, thekua is a selfless offering, a sweet tribute to the Sun God that represents devotion and simplicity.

Chhath Puja: Bihar's Sacred Ritual of Sun Worship

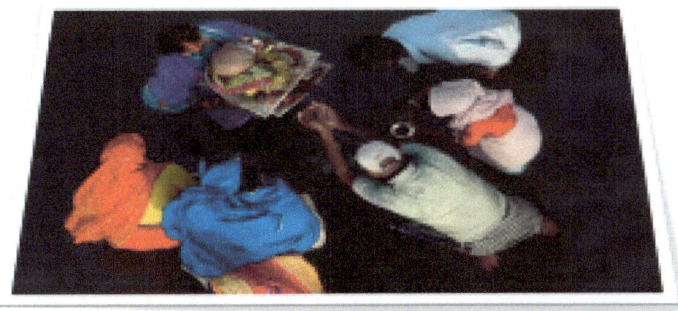

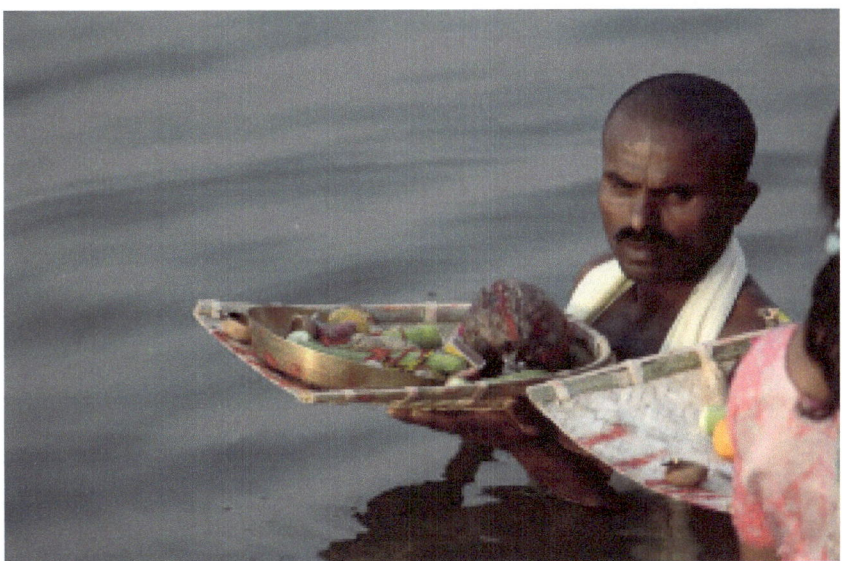

"Fruits, in their untouched simplicity, represent the abundant gifts of nature. By offering these fresh and unaltered gifts, devotees acknowledge the Earth's generosity and seek the Sun God's continued grace."

The array of fresh fruits – bananas, sugarcane, and oranges – symbolizes abundance and gratitude.

Each fruit carries its own significance: bananas for fertility and continuity, sugarcane for sweetness and strength.

These offerings reflect the generosity of the Earth and the devotee's gratitude for sustenance and health.

By presenting these unaltered gifts, worshippers honor the purity of nature's blessings.

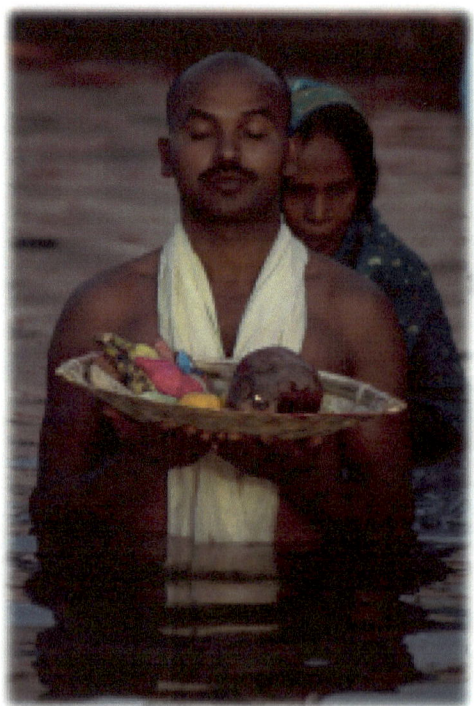

> "Coconuts, pure and unadulterated, represent the steadfast devotion of worshippers. As a symbol of humility and faith, they remind us of the unbreakable bond between the devotee and the divine."

Coconuts, often adorned with sacred threads, represent purity, selflessness, and an open heart.

In Hindu rituals, the coconut is an enduring emblem of devotion and resilience.

For Chhath Puja, coconuts symbolize the devotee's deep connection to the divine, as they are presented with utmost reverence and humility.

Each of these offerings — *thekua*, fruits, and coconuts — collectively reflect the spirit of Chhath Puja: gratitude, simplicity, and unwavering faith in the divine.

They are tokens of devotion, offered with love, and reminders of the sacred bond between humanity and nature.

Chapter 4: Chhath Puja Across Bihar and Beyond

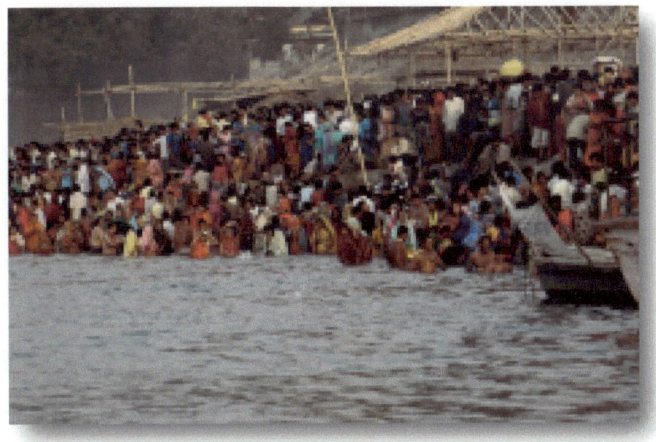

Chhath Puja is not only a festival but a unifying force that transcends regional boundaries and brings people together in shared devotion. While its roots are deeply embedded in Bihar, the festival's significance has spread across various parts of India and even reached the Bihari diaspora worldwide.

This chapter explores how Chhath Puja has evolved and adapted across different regions, maintaining its essence while embracing diverse cultural expressions.

The Heart of Bihar: Regional Variations in Rituals

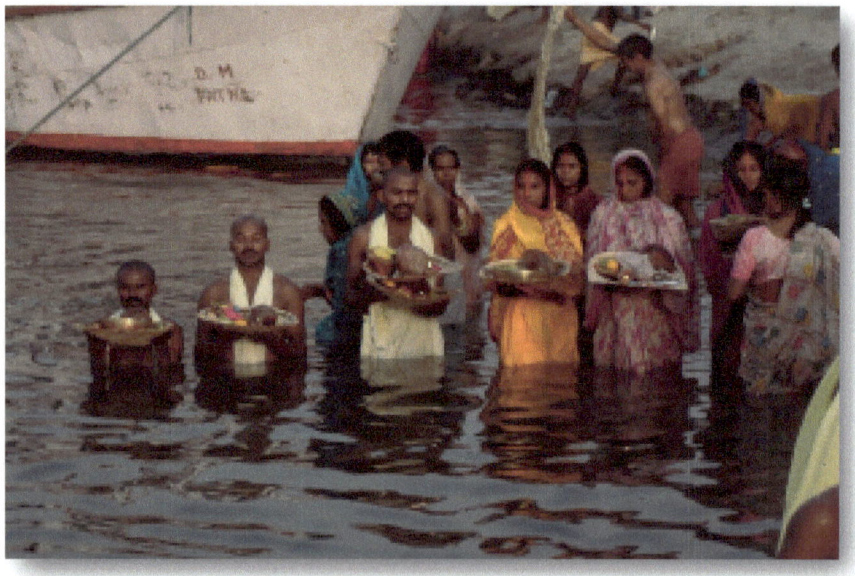

Each region within Bihar brings its own subtle touch to the Chhath Puja rituals, reflecting local customs and traditions.

From the Ghats of Patna, where the banks of the Ganges come alive with the glow of diyas, to the peaceful riversides of small villages where families gather in quiet reverence, the festival's rituals remain both familiar and unique.

In some areas, additional offerings are included, while in others, traditional songs and dances specific to that locality enrich the celebration.

Despite these regional nuances, the heart of Chhath Puja—devotion to the Sun God and gratitude to nature—remains constant across Bihar.

Chhath Puja in the Global Bihari Community

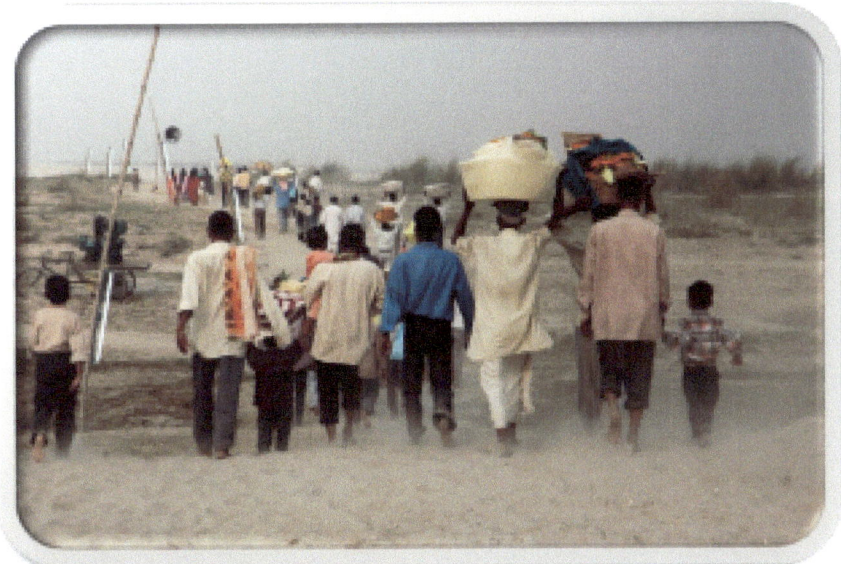

As Bihari communities have settled around the world, Chhath Puja has found its place far beyond Indian borders. In cities across the United States, the United Kingdom, the Middle East, and other parts of the world, Biharis gather by lakes, rivers, and even makeshift water bodies to perform the ancient rituals of Chhath Puja.

These celebrations abroad serve as a bridge to home, connecting families to their roots and heritage, even thousands of miles away.

The festival brings a sense of belonging and continuity, strengthening the cultural identity of the Bihari diaspora while sharing their traditions with other communities globally.

Chapter 5: Traditions and Cultural Significance: The Legacy of Chhath Puja

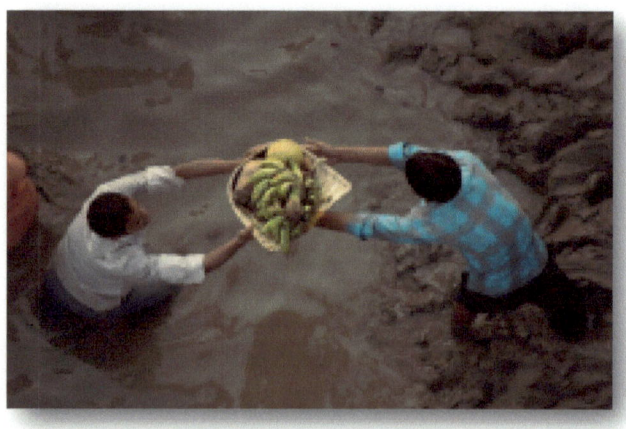

Chhath Puja is steeped in traditions that have been passed down through generations, each ritual a reflection of the values and beliefs of the community.

This chapter delves into the cultural richness of Chhath Puja, exploring the customs that give the festival its depth and timeless relevance.

Chhath Puja: Bihar's Sacred Ritual of Sun Worship

From the preparation of offerings to the symbolic significance of fasting and sun worship, every aspect of Chhath Puja tells a story of reverence and resilience.

Rituals and Customs of Chhath Puja

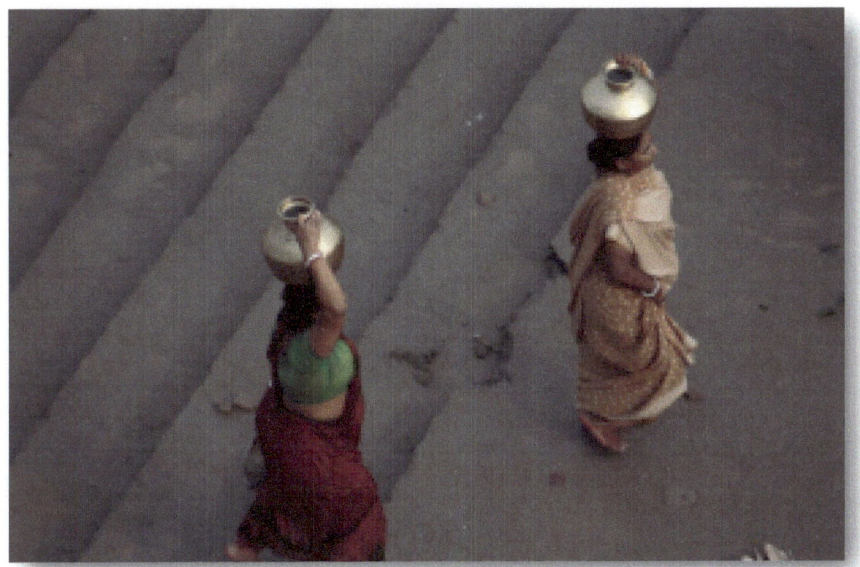

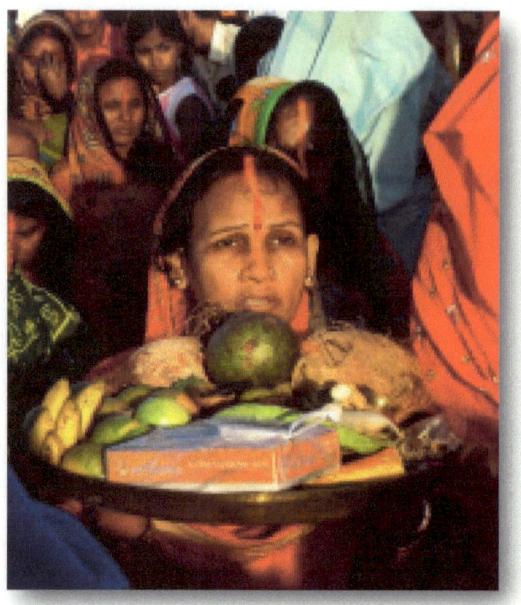

The Power of Fasting: Observing fast during Chhath Puja is not merely an act of devotion but a discipline of mind and body.

The fasting, often lasting for days, is a testament to the worshippers' unwavering faith and commitment, symbolizing purity, patience, and perseverance.

This act of sacrifice is believed to invite the blessings of the Sun God, fostering physical and spiritual strength.

The Offering of Prasad: Each item in the prasad has a deep meaning, from the humble *thekua* to fresh fruits and coconuts.

Prasad is prepared with devotion, using simple ingredients to honor nature's gifts.

The act of offering these items symbolizes gratitude for the earth's abundance, emphasizing the bond between humanity and the natural world.

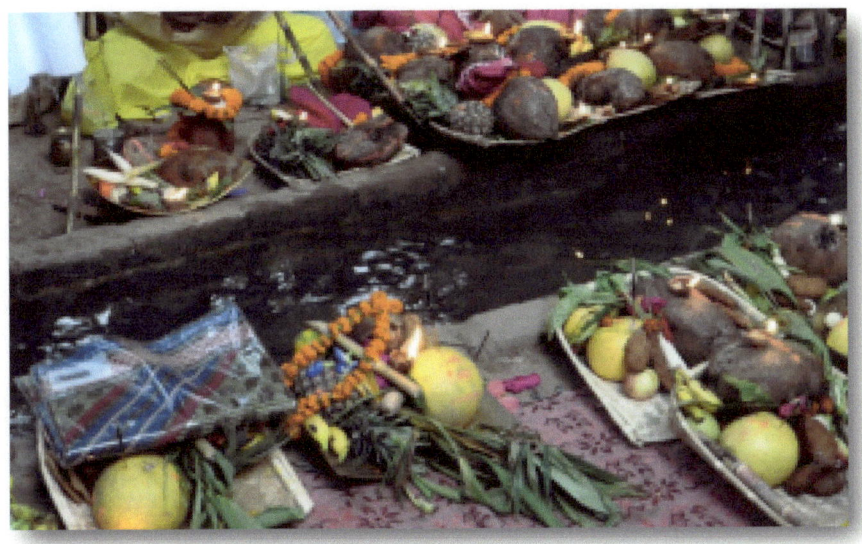

The Role of Family and Community: Chhath Puja is a time when families come together, each member contributing to the rituals.

From preparing the offerings to participating in the sunrise and sunset prayers, every ritual becomes a communal experience.

This unity strengthens familial bonds and reaffirms the sense of belonging and collective faith within the community.

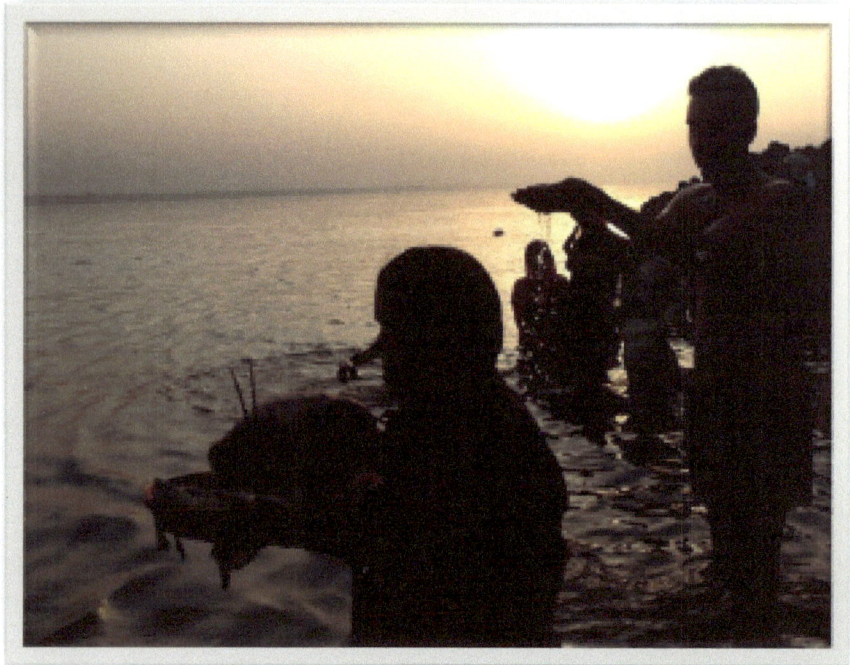

Worship of the Sun: At the heart of Chhath Puja is the worship of the Sun God, a tradition that celebrates life, energy, and sustenance.

The Sun is viewed as a divine force that brings light and warmth to the world, making it central to the rituals.

Both the evening and morning *arghya* to the setting and rising sun signify a harmonious balance between day and night, light and dark, life and rebirth.

Capturing the Spirit of Tradition

Chhath Puja: Bihar's Sacred Ritual of Sun Worship

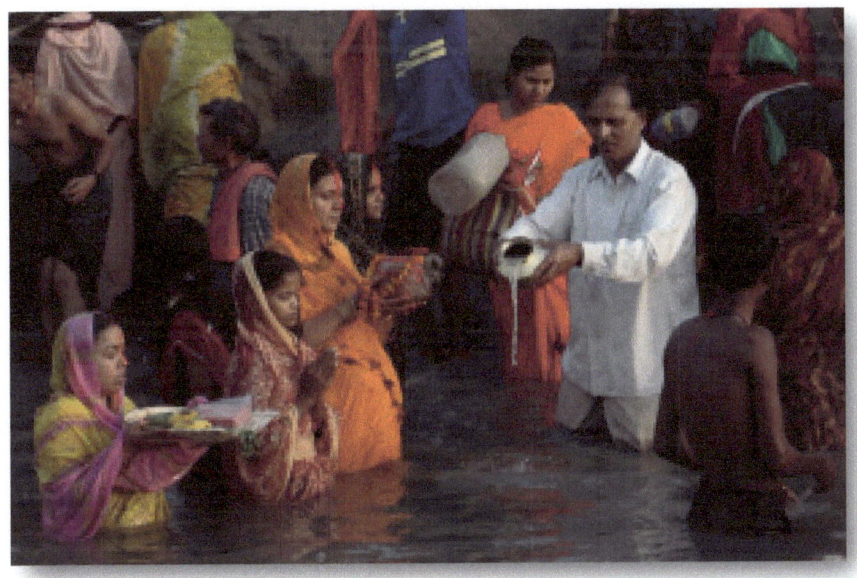

Accompanying the content are visuals that illustrate each aspect of these cherished customs.

Photos of families gathered at the riverbanks, prasad prepared with care, and worshippers standing in reverence capture the essence of Chhath Puja.

These images reflect the legacy of a festival that is as much about personal faith as it is about cultural heritage.

Through these customs, Chhath Puja preserves the collective identity of its devotees, passing down the values of respect, gratitude, and harmony with nature.

Chapter 8: The Environmental and Cultural Impact of Chhath Puja

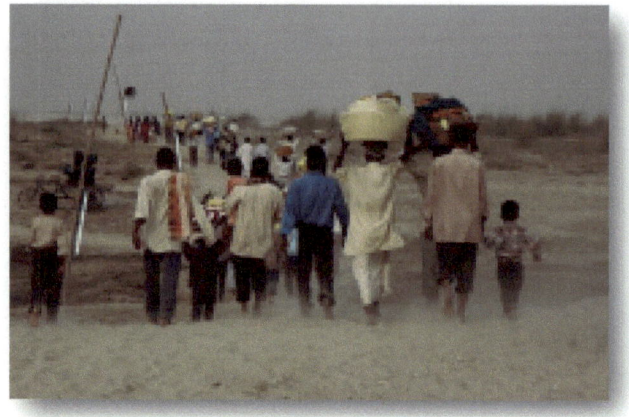

Chhath Puja is more than a religious celebration—it's a powerful reminder of humanity's connection to nature.

Through the rituals performed by water bodies and under open skies, the festival emphasizes harmony with the natural world.

Devotees engage with the environment in a reverent, sustainable way, reflecting on the gifts of the earth and the sun.

This chapter explores how Chhath Puja nurtures environmental awareness and showcases the festival's cultural commitment to respecting and preserving nature.

A Festival Rooted in Natural Spaces

Chhath Puja: Bihar's Sacred Ritual of Sun Worship

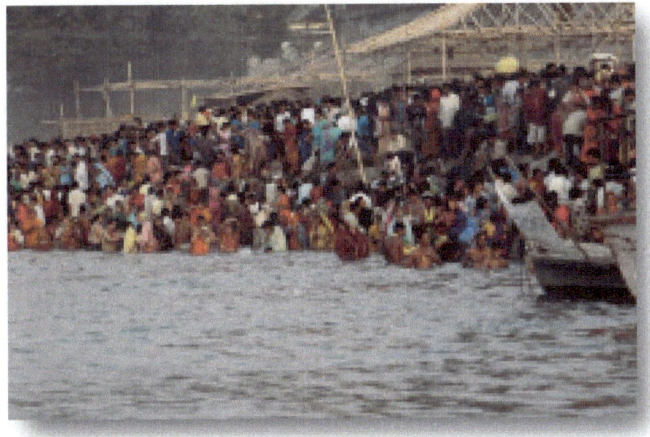

The Sacred Riverbanks: Chhath Puja is often celebrated by riversides and ponds, where worshippers gather to honor the Sun God.

These natural spaces transform into sacred sites, with devotees offering prayers at dawn and dusk, surrounded by the elements of earth and water.

The serene settings highlight the festival's reliance on pure, unspoiled landscapes, reminding participants of their duty to care for these spaces.

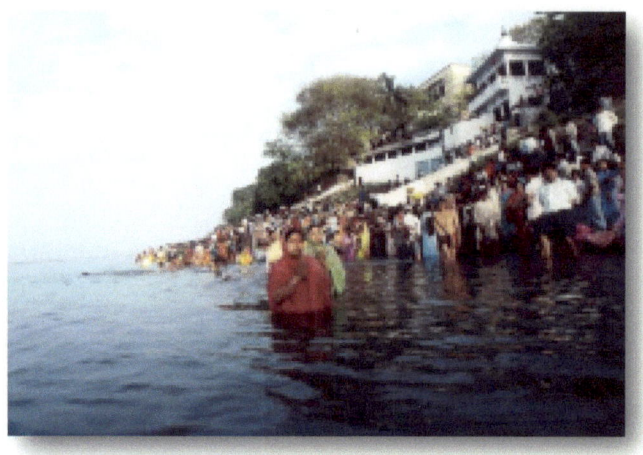

Open Skies and Fresh Waters: The rituals of Chhath Puja are performed under the vast, open sky, symbolizing boundless respect for nature's majesty.

The immersion in rivers, lakes, and ponds during *arghya* is a celebration of water as a life-sustaining force, underscoring the significance of water conservation.

By using natural elements—water, sunlight, and earth—the festival encourages an eco-friendly approach to spirituality.

Chhath Puja: Bihar's Sacred Ritual of Sun Worship

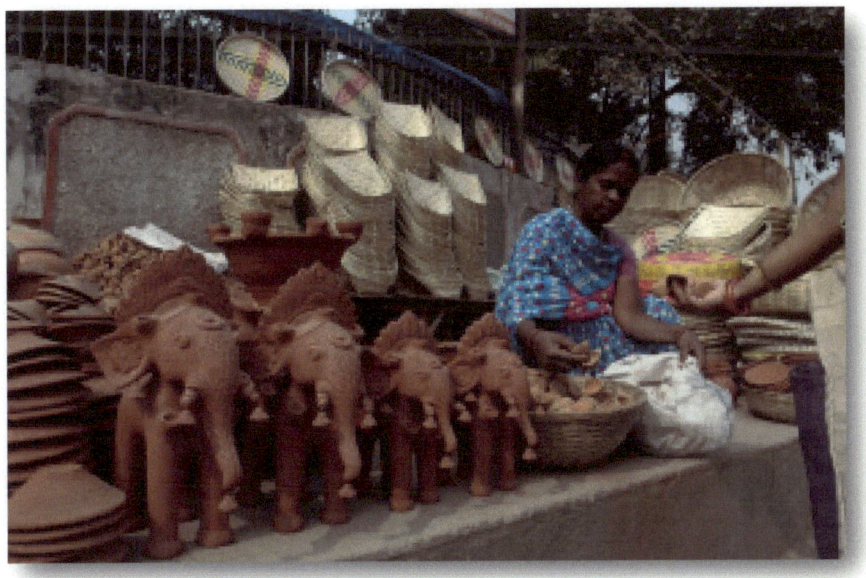

Natural and Minimalist Offerings: Devotees bring offerings that are often locally sourced, such as fresh fruits, earthen pots, and bamboo trays, avoiding synthetic materials that could harm the environment.

This practice aligns with the ethos of sustainability, reinforcing the idea that spirituality and respect for nature go hand in hand.

Water Bodies and Environmental Consciousness

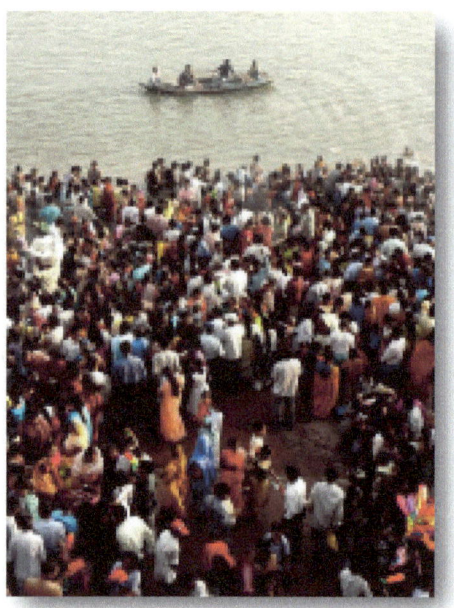

Water holds a sacred place in Chhath Puja, not only as a ritual element but also as a symbol of life, purity, and sustainability.

Devotees gather at rivers, ponds, and lakes to perform the rituals, which elevates these water bodies to spiritual sanctuaries.

This tradition fosters a deep respect for water as a precious resource, encouraging participants to protect and preserve it.

By choosing natural locations for worship, Chhath Puja promotes environmental consciousness and sustainable practices, as devotees are reminded of the importance of clean, unpolluted water for both the ritual and their everyday lives.

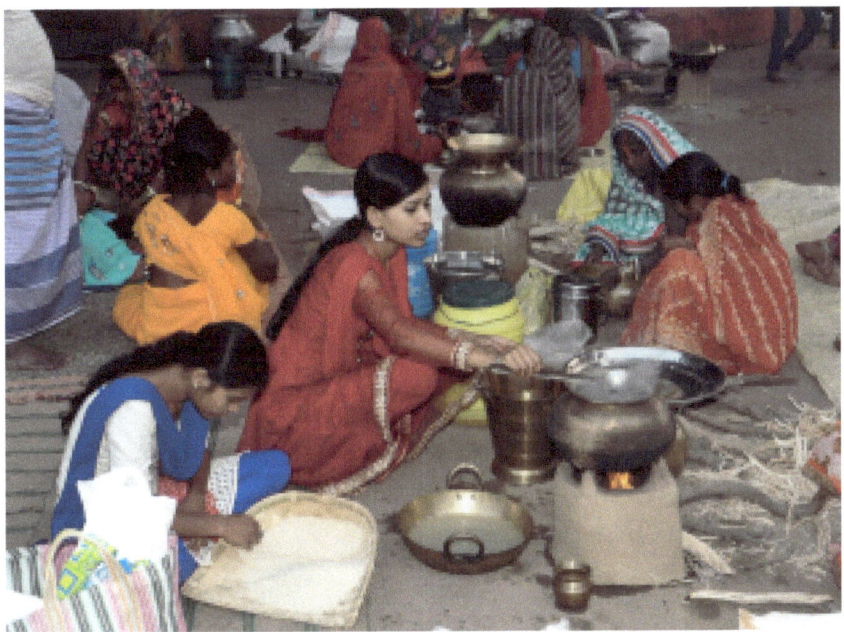

Beyond its environmental significance, Chhath Puja has a cultural impact that strengthens community bonds and reinforces the values of respect and gratitude for the earth.

By integrating nature into its rituals, the festival serves as a cultural bridge between ancient beliefs and modern environmental awareness.

Each act, from offering food to the river to the mindful use of organic materials, reinforces a message of coexistence with nature.

Through these practices, Chhath Puja becomes a festival of ecological harmony, celebrating both the physical and spiritual sustenance provided by the natural world.

Conclusion and Final Reflection

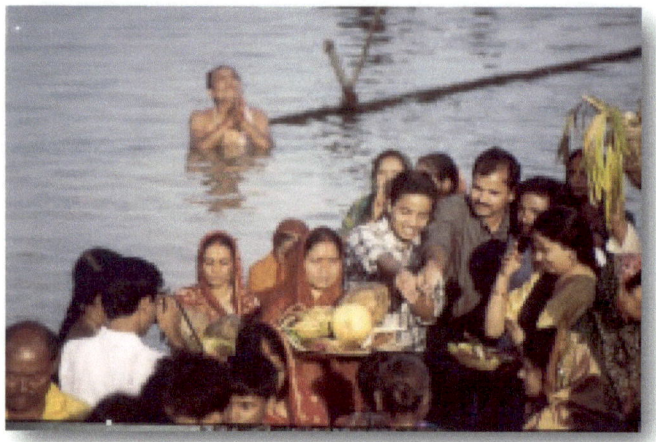

Chhath Puja stands as a timeless celebration, embodying the resilience of tradition and the beauty of human connection with nature.

Its rituals, performed with devotion and gratitude, are a powerful reminder of the harmony between humanity and the natural world.

Year after year, devotees return to the water's edge, honoring the Sun God and expressing reverence for life's blessings.

In a world that constantly evolves, Chhath Puja remains a steadfast symbol of faith, community, and ecological awareness.

This festival is more than a ritual; it is a legacy passed down through generations.

Each offering, every prayer, and each moment spent by the river connects devotees to their roots, reminding them of the values of humility, patience, and reverence for nature.

Chhath Puja: Bihar's Sacred Ritual of Sun Worship

In celebrating Chhath Puja, communities reaffirm their commitment to these principles, ensuring that the wisdom of the past continues to illuminate the present.

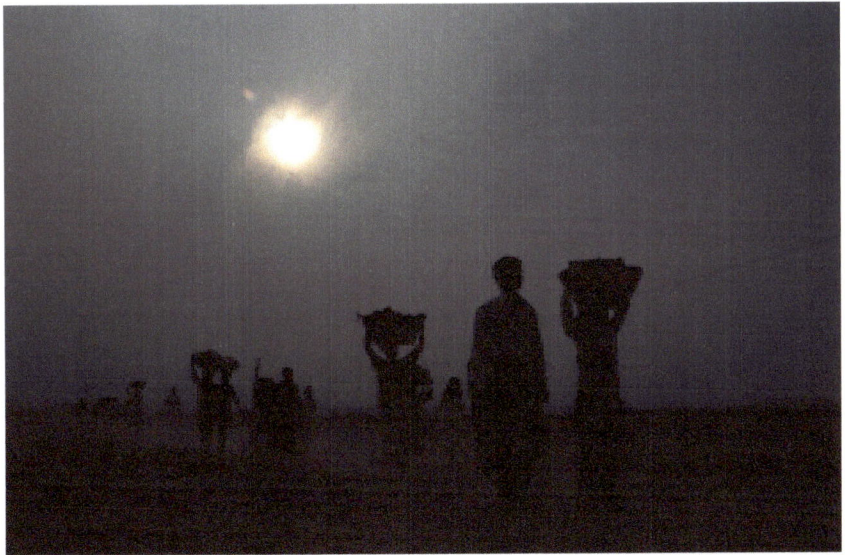

In this final reflection, we see that Chhath Puja's essence lies in its simplicity and sincerity.

The rising sun not only marks the end of the ritual but also symbolizes new beginnings, the cyclical beauty of life, and the shared faith of millions.

> "Chhath Puja is, at its core, a festival of unity and hope—a tradition that endures and inspires, shining brightly in the hearts of those who honor it."

Acknowledgments

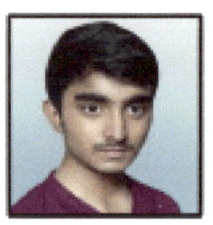

Tanmay Sinha

(Editor)

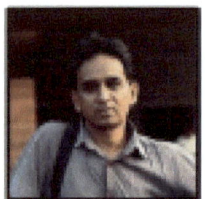

Manish Sinha

(Author and Photographer)

This book is the result of shared efforts, unwavering support, and a deep passion for honoring the sacred traditions of Chhath Puja. My heartfelt gratitude goes to the many devotees who celebrate this festival each year, offering their wisdom and preserving the beauty of this cultural legacy. I would also like to thank everyone who contributed their insights and encouragement throughout the creation of this book.

Special thanks to my editor, Tanmay Sinha, for his invaluable guidance and dedication, ensuring that each page reflects the spirit and significance of Chhath Puja. I am also grateful to my family and friends, whose constant support and enthusiasm have inspired this work. To all those who continue to honor and celebrate Chhath Puja, this book is dedicated to you.

About the Author and Photographer

Manish Sinha is a passionate photographer and writer dedicated to capturing and sharing the vibrant traditions and cultural heritage of India. With a deep connection to Bihar and its customs, Manish brings Chhath Puja to life through evocative photography and storytelling. His work is inspired by the faith and resilience of the communities who preserve these sacred rituals, and he hopes this book will serve as a lasting tribute to their devotion.

Tanmay Sinha, editor of this book, has played a key role in shaping its narrative and ensuring the essence of Chhath Puja shines through each page. Tanmay's eye for detail and his commitment to authenticity have made this work a true reflection of the festival's significance. Together, Manish and Tanmay are proud to present this homage to Chhath Puja, celebrating its timeless beauty and enduring legacy.

www.ingramcontent.com/pod-product-compliance
Lightning Source LLC
Chambersburg PA
CBHW040241220526
45473CB00001B/325